Everything You Need To Know About

# ANGER

Anger can be a destructive force if it is not controlled.

# • THE NEED TO KNOW LIBRARY •

## Everything You Need To Know About

# ANGER

### Renora Licata

THE ROSEN PUBLISHING GROUP, INC.
NEW YORK

Published in 1992 by The Rosen Publishing Group, Inc.
29 East 21st Street, New York, NY 10010

First Edition
Copyright 1992 by The Rosen Publishing Group, Inc.

Printed in Canada

**Library of Congress Cataloging-in-Publication Data**

Licata, Renora
    Everything you need to know about anger/ Renora Licata.—1st
ed.
    (The Need to know library)
    Includes bibliographical references and index.
    Summary: Discusses the causes of anger and its ill effects on
people, as well as ways to control it.
    ISBN 0-8239-1320-1
    1. Anger—Juvenile literature. [1. Anger.] I. Title. II. Series.
BF575.A5L53   1991
152.4'7—dc20                     91-14358
                                               CIP
                                                 AC

# Contents

# Introduction

"When angry, count four; when very angry, swear."
—*Mark Twain*

**D**id you ever get really upset at something? Did you ever get mad enough to scream out loud, or slam a door? Maybe you threw a book across the room. Did you ever turn quickly away from someone? All of these actions show anger.

We all know anger. Anger is a strong feeling. You are full of many different kinds of feelings. These feelings are called *emotions*. Some of them are comfortable, and some are uncomfortable.

As infants, we are allowed to scream and cry to have our needs met.
As adults, we must communicate in other ways.

Many people agree that there are about eight basic emotions—fear, joy, sadness, acceptance, disgust, surprise, curiosity, and anger.  These are normal feelings.  They are the emotions you feel every day. They make up an important part of your personality.  They also help others to understand you.

Take a closer look at anger.  Some questions come to mind right away.  "What is anger?" "Is our anger always harmful?" "Do nice people get angry?" "Why do some people get mad more easily than others?" "How do we control our anger?" These are some of the things we will be talking about in this book.

Anger is a strong feeling of displeasure.  It is the way you react to someone or something you truly dislike. Getting angry is also a natural reaction to feeling threatened.

You have been making decisions since you were born.  You knew what you liked, what made you happy.  You also knew what you didn't like, what made you mad!  You responded to the world around you mostly from *instinct.*  Instinct is the ability to act naturally.  Instinctive behavior is acting in ways you did not learn from anyone.

When you were a baby, whenever you were upset you probably needed to "let it out."  By fussing or crying, you were sending a message to those around you:  "I am not happy.  I need your help." We send messages like those all our lives.  Our words and actions express our feelings.  Even the ways we move our bodies often show our likes and dislikes.

Feeling angry is not a bad thing. Expressing anger does not have to be hurtful. The feeling of anger is not your enemy. In fact, when anger is kept under control, it can be used as a warning signal. It tells you that something is not quite right. When you feel angry, you must do something to change what is upsetting you. Then you will begin to feel better again.

Reading this book can help you do some important things for yourself:

- Understand your anger and the reason for it.
- Learn to express your anger in acceptable ways.
- Work on changing some things that make you angry.
- Cope with your anger when problems arise that cannot be changed.

Keep in mind that feelings *in themselves* are never wrong. If anger is what you are feeling, that's okay. The important thing is what you *do* when you are angry. It is your actions that may affect others.

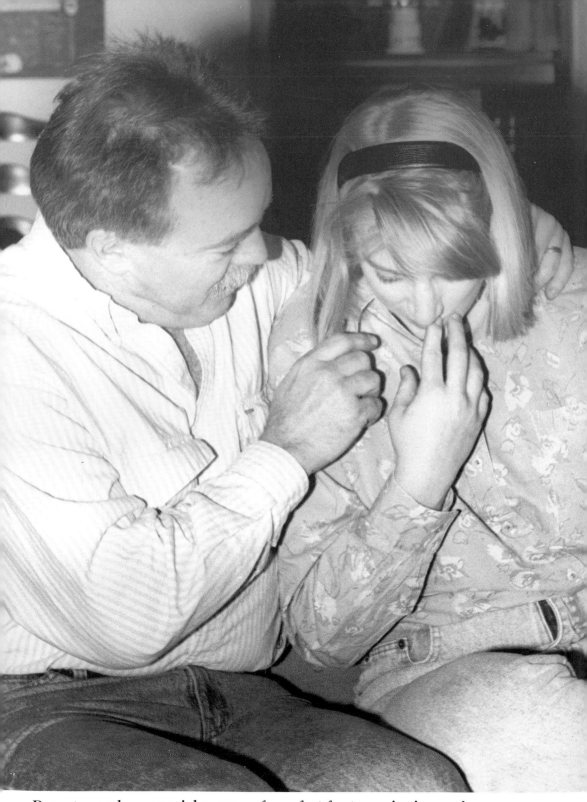

Parents can be a special source of comfort for teens in times of frustration, anger, and confusion.

# Chapter 1

---

# Why Do You Feel
# So Angry?

Anger is a strong feeling of displeasure. It is an emotion that comes from within you. Anger can arise suddenly, without warning. It can also build up slowly over a period of time. When you feel angry you are reacting to someone or something you dislike. You are uncomfortable.

## It's Not Nice

We all have angry feelings from time to time. That is normal. The hard part is keeping these feelings under control. Sometimes these feelings are stronger than at other times. Because we are different, we all express our feelings in our own ways. Some studies show that you may inherit certain traits from your parents. These traits may influence your ability to feel emotion and express it.

*11*

Anger is sometimes misunderstood. While growing up, you may have gotten confusing messages about anger and angry feelings. Most parents teach their children at an early age how important it is to be nice. That is the accepted behavior. If you stick out your tongue at your brother, your mother tells you, "That's not nice." If you laugh when someone trips and falls, you hear about it: "Shame on you. Nice boys and girls don't do that."

Think back to those times when you raised your voice in anger. How quickly were you stopped? "That's no way to behave!" Did you think you were expected to be nice all the time? How was that possible?

Did you think any of these things when
　　you were younger?

- It is wrong to feel or express anger.
- Only bad people get angry and show their
　　temper.
- If you get angry, nobody will like you or
　　want to be with you.

How do you feel about anger now?

- Do you keep your feelings to yourself?
- Do you feel guilty when you feel angry at
　　someone?
- Do you stay away from people who are
　　more open about their feelings?

## It's Scary

An angry person can get out of control. That can be very frightening. A very angry grown-up can be very scary when you are a child. You don't know what will happen next. You are scared that someone will be hurt. The person in danger may be someone you love. It may be you. You feel helpless. That feeling can make you angry. You may be surprised at how strong your own angry feelings can get.

*Billy promised himself that he would never stand by and watch his father hit his mother again. Billy loved them both, but he knew his father was wrong. Billy was afraid. He would stop the hitting the next time. He didn't care how. Billy thought about stopping his father for good! That scared him even more.*

Billy isn't a bad boy. He hates what is happening to his mother. He is confused. His anger is making him think about hurting his father. He doesn't know what to do.

When something makes you feel scared and angry, like Billy, you need help. Find an adult you can talk to. That may be a teacher, a priest or rabbi, a social worker, or family member. Tell the adult what is going on. If the person you tell does not believe you, tell someone else. Keep telling people you trust until you find someone who will help. It's hard to deal with such strong emotions alone.

## Feeling Stress

*Jeff's older brother, Pete, had gone off to college. His parents were still talking about how well Pete had done in high school. They said it was Pete's fast ball pitch that had kept the baseball team in first place for two years. They remembered how nice it had been having Pete's friends around the house.*

*Jeff had different interests than Pete. He played lead guitar in his own hard rock group. He loved rock music and hoped to write songs someday. He wanted his parents to like him as much as they liked Pete. But they always told him to "keep the noise down" when he rehearsed. And couldn't he and the guys go somewhere else? Jeff was also nervous when his parents were around. He hated the way they talked to him.*

*Lisa was upset. It was hard for her to adjust to a new high school in her junior year. This new school was much bigger. And no one seemed friendly. She missed her old friends. Lisa moped around the house all the time. She didn't really try to make new friends. She never had a kind word for anyone.*

Both Jeff and Lisa were feeling *stressed*. Stress is a feeling of being pressured in some way. Jeff felt his parents were not satisfied with him. Lisa knew she had to "fit in" at her new school. There was no going back. For Jeff and Lisa, stress was the beginning of angry feelings. They were angry with their families for making them uncomfortable.

Children learn much about dealing with anger by watching their parents.

More and more studies show that stress can be unhealthy. After a while, stress can lead to strong anger. Do you feel angry most of the time? Maybe something in your life is causing you stress. Learning to recognize the warning signals of stress is important. When you can identify your feelings, you can control them.

Here are some of the ways that stress can make you feel. Have you felt any of these feelings lately?

- Irritable, cross, crabby
- Tired, restless
- Jumpy, excitable, "wired"
- Upset stomach, nervous
- Paranoid
- Having strong feelings about minor problems
- Confused, unable to concentrate
- Doubting your ability
- Smiling less

Don't keep things to yourself. Talk to someone who can help you sort out your feelings. Make a list of ways to relieve your stress. Maybe exercising, reading, watching TV, or listening to a favorite tape would help. When you are calm you can think clearly. When you are relaxed, you will see other choices for dealing with your problems.

# CONSTANT ANGER: A HAZARD TO HEALTH

When you get angry, your body produces certain chemicals. These chemicals get your body ready for a "fight." They make your heart beat faster and make you feel warmer. They raise blood pressure and cause heavy breathing. They are trying to help you react to stress.

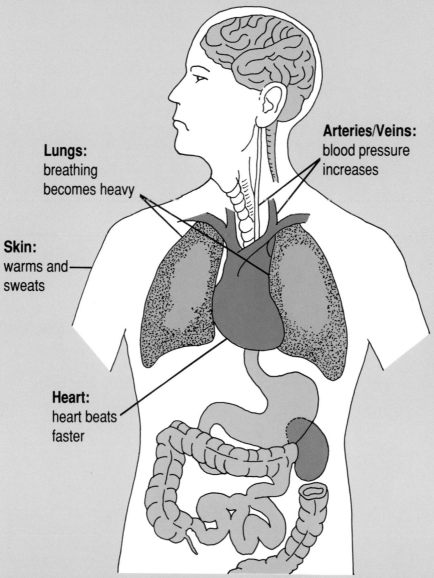

**Lungs:**
breathing
becomes heavy

**Arteries/Veins:**
blood pressure
increases

**Skin:**
warms and
sweats

**Heart:**
heart beats
faster

People who are always angry are always producing these "fight" chemicals. That means their bodies are under constant stress. After a while, this stress can harm the body. Among other things, the heart can become weak and the arteries can become stiff, from constant high blood pressure.

## Feeling Threatened

*Ramon does not do drugs. But Ramon is afraid for his younger brother, Juan. Drugs are hard to resist. The drug dealers are on the streets in his neighborhood. Drug dealers are even in his school.*

*Juan likes to buy nice things. Juan knows some kids that sell drugs. They always have lots of money to spend. They keep bothering Juan. They want him to "push" drugs too.*

*Ramon loves his brother. It makes him feel angry when these dealers pester Juan. Juan may not be strong enough to say "no."*

*Tara and Steve had been dating for two years. They were often together in school. One day Tara told Steve that she wanted to break up with him. She wanted to date other boys. Steve was very upset. He would not let her go. He hassled Tara at school. He started calling her at home late at night and wouldn't stop asking her why she was being so mean. He followed her wherever she went.*

*Tara was afraid. Steve had never acted so "crazy" before. It made her feel angry.*

When you feel someone or something may cause you harm, you are feeling *threatened*. This harm could be to your body. It could be to your *self-esteem*. (Self-esteem is how you feel about yourself). Or it could be harm to people, places, or things that have special meaning for you. Feeling threatened can lead to angry feelings.

Ramon felt that the drug dealers were a serious threat to his brother. Selling or using drugs is very harmful. This threat made Ramon feel angry.

For Tara, Steve became the threat. He continued to bother her. Soon, Tara felt that Steve might be a threat to her safety. This led to her angry feelings. And it led to Tara becoming irritable and nervous.

## Feeling Frustrated

*Terrance couldn't believe that he didn't make the varsity basketball team. Since last season's disappointment, he had practiced long hours each week. But he still didn't even make the first cut. He had even grown an inch or two! All his dreams were shattered in one afternoon. He became so angry. He started yelling at the coach right in the middle of their first practice. He told his friends how stupid they were to waste their time playing ball. Then he stormed out of the gym.*

*Rosa really wanted to go to the Spring dance. Most of her friends already had dates. No one had asked her yet. She was feeling disappointed and unpopular. Her self-esteem was hitting bottom. She decided the only thing to do was to invite someone. She tried but three boys turned her down. Rosa was miserable! She cried a lot and felt sorry for herself. She avoided her friends. Any talk of the dance just made her angry.*

Writing down the things that make you angry is one way to help you stay in control of your emotions.

A person feels *frustration* when he or she cannot do something that is important to him or her. Terrance and Rosa felt frustrated. They had set goals for themselves. Terrance wanted to be on the varsity team. Rosa wanted to go to the dance. They both worked for what they wanted. They both failed to reach their goals. It is never easy to accept defeat. It can make you angry.

Teenage years are difficult. Many changes are taking place. Your emotions are changing with the rest of your body. You are exploring new feelings. These changes are not bad. They are necessary for your development. Changes mean that there are new things to understand about yourself. If you are feeling angry, look closely at your other feelings as well. Ask yourself:

- Am I under stress of any kind?
- Do I feel threatened somehow?
- Is someone (or something) important to me at risk?
- Do I feel frustrated, discouraged?
- Am I setting realistic goals for myself?
- Am I thinking about my failure in the wrong way?

Answer these questions first. You may be able to understand why you are feeling angry. Finding out the reason why you're angry can be the most important step. It can keep you in control. It can help you feel like you have the power to solve your problems.

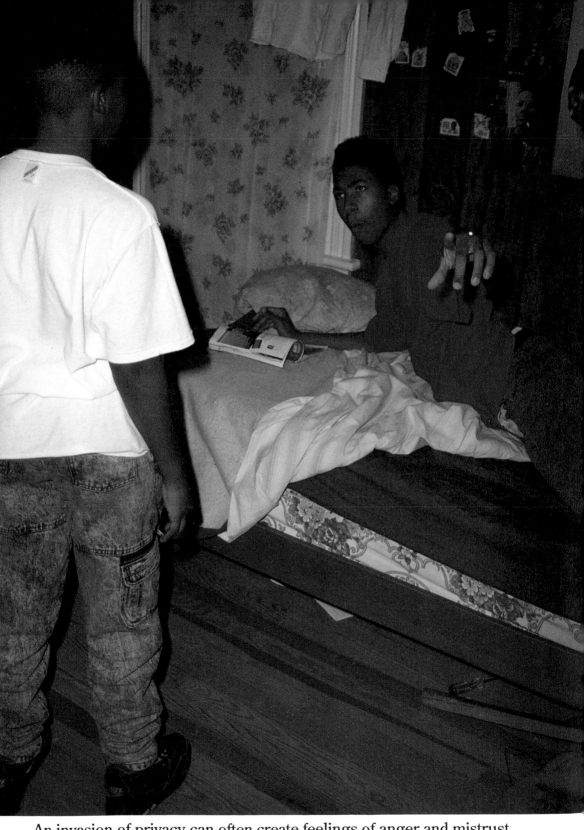

An invasion of privacy can often create feelings of anger and mistrust.

# Chapter 2

## Anger That Can Help

Do you believe that feeling angry may help you solve a problem? Sometimes it can. Sometimes you feel that your anger is *justified*. That means you believe there is a good reason for it. Justified anger may help you to start thinking about what is right and wrong. It may get you to gather your courage. It may make you feel brave. It may help you to take action and change things.

### Dawn's Story

The following story is about a common problem that threatens young women. As you read about Dawn, try to understand what she is feeling.

*Dawn is 14. Her family is very friendly with the Martin family. She baby-sits regularly for the Martins. At the end of the evening Mr. Martin always drives her home.*

*One night, Mr. Martin started talking to Dawn during the ride home. The way he was talking made her feel uncomfortable.*

*"You have grown up a lot this past year, Dawn. In fact, I never realized just how sexy you are." He placed his hand on her leg for a moment, then added, "I always enjoy having you around."*

*Dawn felt a little strange and embarrassed. Mr. Martin never talked this way before. She had known him all her life. She always thought he was fun. For the next few days, Dawn kept thinking about what Mr. Martin had said. After a while, she decided that she was just being silly. Mr. Martin was an old friend of the family. He was a trusted adult. Dawn decided there was no reason to worry.*

*The following weekend, Dawn baby-sat again. Everything seemed fine until she was in the car driving home. Mr. Martin was not going the usual way. Dawn asked him where he was taking her. He said it would be nice to take a little ride. Dawn thanked him, but said she was tired and wanted to go right home. Mr. Martin paid no attention to what she said. He drove a few more blocks, then parked the car in a hidden lot near the city's public tennis courts.*

*Before Dawn could say anything, Mr. Martin leaned over and kissed her. Dawn was shocked! Her*

A happy, supportive family can provide strength for members during times of stress.

*heart was beating very fast.  She pushed Mr. Martin away and told him to stop.  He grabbed her and kissed her harder on the mouth and neck.  Again, she broke free and tried to get out of the car.  He held her back then pulled her close.  "Leave me alone," Dawn screamed at him.  "What's the matter with you?"*

*"Take it easy, Dawn.  You know I'd never hurt you.  Just relax, and we can have some fun."*

*Dawn kept insisting that Mr. Martin let her go. "Okay, okay," he said.  "If you don't try to get out of the car, I'll drive you home.  Maybe next time you will be in a better mood."*

*Dawn cried when she was back home alone in her room.  She was confused.  She was not sure what she should do.  She lay awake most of the night.  It made her feel angry to think that Mr. Martin would hurt her.  She had always thought of him as a friend.  She liked him.  She trusted him.  But he had broken that trust.  Dawn knew she had done nothing wrong.  Mr. Martin had ruined their friendship.  Things could never be the same.  It was all his fault.*

*In the morning, Dawn decided to tell her dad everything that had happened.  She knew that he would be surprised and upset too.  But he would know the right way to handle the problem.*

*After they talked things over, Dawn gave her dad a big hug.  He told her how sorry he was that this had happened.  And he told her she had done the right thing by telling him.  Dawn's dad made sure that Mr. Martin never bothered his daughter again.*

Things turned out okay for Dawn. She was brave. Dawn knew there was good reason to be angry with Mr. Martin. She did not ignore her feelings. She did not try to hide them either. Dawn expressed her anger in acceptable ways. She kept her feelings under control, but she acted quickly. She got the help and support she needed.

## What You Can Do

Taking steps yourself to solve a problem is a good feeling. When you get angry, your feelings become very strong. Like Dawn, you can use that strength to:

- express yourself
- get help for yourself (or others)
- make changes for the better
- become more independent
- feel good about yourself

Learn to trust your feelings. There may be a good reason for you to be feeling angry. Think of *anger that helps* as a "call to action," a chance to get involved. You cannot solve every problem in your life. Things will not always be fair or easy. But when you stay in control and try hard, sometimes there is a way out. Things can change for the better. And you may make the difference by using your emotions in a positive way!

Anger can sometimes cause people to become physically aggressive in order to have their way.

# Chapter 3

# Anger That Can Hurt

There are different kinds of anger. In this chapter we will talk about anger that can be *destructive.* That means anger that hurts people or things. This kind of anger is unacceptable. It is usually out of control. It can destroy feelings, friendships, love, and lives.

How can you tell when your anger (or someone else's) is destructive? To help you decide, look closely at:

- the intensity (strength) of the anger
- how long it lasts
- how it is expressed
- who or what it affects
- if it hurts the angry person, other people, or physical things

Here is an example: Your sister accidentally breaks the new stereo you got for your birthday. Do you "blow up"? Do you scream and holler and call her names? Do you tell her to stay out of your room? Or do you slowly "burn" and then walk straight to her room and rip her posters off the wall? And then unwind all her music tapes? Which response do you think is more fitting for something that was not done on purpose?

## Violence

Violence is an expression of very strong feelings. Violence means using physical force to injure or abuse someone or something. Violence is a choice some people make when they are angry. We read about violence in the newspapers and watch it on TV every day.

Victims of violence are people of all ages. Violence happens in the home, in school, and on the streets. A victim of violence can suffer mentally as well as physically. The effects of violence can last a long time.

Some kinds of anger can cause violent behavior:

- *Rage* is an intense anger that is uncontrollable.
- *Fury* is a kind of rage that looks like madness.
- *Wrath* is a powerful anger that makes you want to punish someone or get even.

Sometimes "letting it all out" is the best way to release anger, as long as it is not harmful to yourself or others.

These angry feelings can come suddenly, without warning. Or they can build up slowly over a period of time. A person can easily get carried away and lose control. There is no way to predict the actions of a person with this much anger.

## "Losing It"

When someone "loses it" it means they are "letting it all out." This can be either emotional or physical, or both. This kind of anger can also be hurtful. The purpose of this kind of anger is to "let off steam." Sometimes it means the person is out of control. Here are some examples:

- Throwing a temper tantrum if you don't get your way.
- Slamming doors to let your parents know you don't like their rules.
- Yelling and swearing if you hit your thumb with a hammer.
- Driving recklessly trying to catch the car that cut you off.

Anger of this kind can be hard to handle. It is best to go off by yourself when your feelings become too strong to control. Find a private place to "explode." Scream, kick, jump up and down, or punch at something. Do whatever it takes to calm down *without* hurting yourself or anyone else.

## Other Destructive Behavior

Some kinds of behavior come from hidden anger. This kind of anger is not easy to identify.

Sometimes when people are angry they spread *gossip* about others. Gossiping is telling others very personal things about someone you know. People can be very unkind with words. Even if the story you tell is true, feelings can be hurt.

Gossip may betray a trust. It may be a trust between friends, sisters, brothers, neighbors, or a parent and child.

*Criticism* means finding fault with someone or something. Sometimes angry people express themselves this way. Children need to be told when they make mistakes or make poor choices. But too much criticism by an adult can make a child feel "put down" or stupid.

The "silent treatment" may be anger used to control. The angry person blocks all communication. He or she has the power to decide *when* and *if* things will get back to normal again. The other person feels hurt, frustrated, and helpless.

Sometimes a person will hold a *grudge* against another person. He or she will not forget or forgive the other person. The anger and bad feelings can last for a long time, even years.

Have you ever heard the expression: "If looks could kill...?" A nasty look or violent gesture can also send a message of intense anger. Even without harsh words, anger can hurt others.

## Anger Turned Inward

Many mental health experts agree that anger turned inward (on ourselves) is our worst enemy. You listen to that little voice inside you that says you are a failure. You begin to believe that you cannot do anything right. It scares you. You don't like yourself very much. You are not able to enjoy the things you used to do. Many times you choose to be alone. Your *self-esteem* is getting lower.

*Depression* is often the next step. Depression means feeling very low. Depressed people can be old or young. They stop taking an interest in everyday life. They may not care how they look, what they eat, or what they do. It can affect their body and mind. Sometimes depressed people can become seriously ill. Sometimes their mind plays tricks on them, and they imagine that they are ill. Depression can go on for a long time.

As depression and poor self-esteem get worse, behavior gets more *self-destructive.* When people don't feel valuable, they make poor choices in their lives. They stop caring. They may turn to alcohol, drugs, sex, crime, or suicide as a way out.

All of these social problems are increasing. And statistics show that more and more young people are getting into trouble at an earlier age. Anger that causes someone to act in hurtful ways is disturbing. It is especially sad when a young person is involved.

# Chapter 4

# Living with Angry People

Any constant group of related people makes up a *family*. The person or people you live with are your family. A family may include a mother and/or father, stepparents, stepsiblings, sisters, brothers, cousins, or grandparents.

## Learning from Family

Your family has the greatest influence on you. You learn many things from them. You are taught at home how to behave and how to treat other people. You learn the value of things like responsibility, honesty, and courage. You learn to make your own decisions and deal with your own problems. In many ways, the kind of person you become depends largely upon your family. And, just as important, your family affects how you feel about yourself.

A healthy family fulfills certain needs for its members:

- the need to be loved
- the need for support and encouragement
- the need to express yourself
- the need to feel safe and secure.

Even in the best of families, things are not always perfect. Family members do not always have to agree with each other. But they care about each other. They try to work things out. The adults in a healthy family provide good *role models* for their children. A role model is someone who serves as an example for others.

## A Special Problem

All children deserve a happy, healthy family— one that loves them, teaches them, and makes them feel good about themselves. What happens to children when their family life is *not* happy? When the people they depend on let them down? When they feel afraid in their own home?

Let's read one family's story.

*Kevin and Mike's father has been out of work since his company moved two years ago. He had worked there for 18 years. That was the only job he ever had. It is hard for him to look for a new one. These days, he stays at home and watches TV most of the time. He is usually in a bad mood. Every little thing starts a major argument.*

Being out of work for a long time can make a person feel like a failure.

*Kevin and Mike's mother has been working two part- time jobs. Their father still complains about her. He says that the house is always a mess and his dinner is never on time. The boys' parents hardly even speak to each other. The mother is too tired to argue. She hates the way her husband treats her. She knows how unhappy he is, but it makes her angry to see him hang around every day. She is sure there is work he can do somewhere. If only he would try!*

*Kevin is a sensitive boy about 14 years old. He feels sorry that his father lost his job. He likes to remember the good times they used to have together. Now there is a lot of yelling and silent anger around the house. It makes Kevin feel nervous and unhappy most of the time.*

*Kevin is a hard worker. He has a job delivering newspapers. He also does well in school. He talks to his mother about his plans for college someday. She is proud of her son. She knows Kevin tries hard to be helpful and cheerful. He does not want to upset his father.*

*The older brother, Mike, spends most of his time with his friends. He doesn't have much interest in anything. He hates school. And he wants to drop out of school as soon as he turns 16. Mike only thinks about drinking with the guys and having a good time. Even when he is home, he stays up in his room. He does not want to deal with his father's problems. Most of the time he blasts his stereo so loud that it blocks out the other sounds in the house.*

This family is feeling the stress and frustration of having a parent out of work. The father's anger may be hiding some of his other feelings. He may be afraid he will be turned down for a job he really wants. He may be embarrassed to take a lower-level job. And he may feel he is less of a man because his wife works to support the family.

This father is not a positive role model for his sons. Losing his job was not his fault, but he has given up looking for work. That has made matters worse. The more time that passes, the more depressed and helpless he feels. And his anger grows. His behavior becomes more destructive for himself and his family.

Kevin feels sad that things at home are not happy the way they used to be. He may not fully understand, but he doesn't blame anyone. He is close to his mother and needs her love and support. She has helped him to continue to feel good about himself. Kevin is coping with a difficult home life in a positive way. He believes in himself. He looks to the future. He has learned to accept what he cannot change at home.

Mike, on the other hand, has let his friends take the place of his family. He is not coping with his family problems. He simply avoids them. Mike is not being honest with himself. He pretends that a "good time" is all he needs. What he really needs is

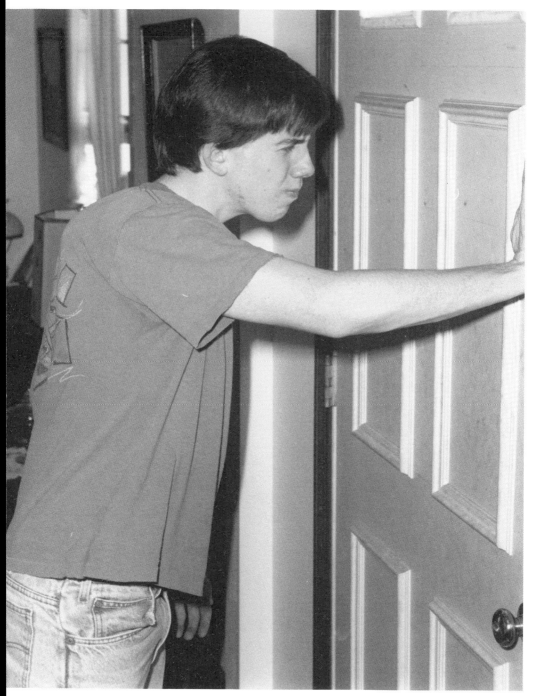

Controlling a desire to be destructive while angry is important for all teens to learn.

a responsible adult to talk to.  Mike does not feel as close to his mother as Kevin does. So he must go outside the family for help.  He must find someone to help him understand what he is feeling. He must learn to express his feelings in acceptable ways. Then he may start to feel better.

Is there too much anger in your family?  Are you learning destructive ways to behave?  Are you in danger in your own home?  If you answer "yes" to any of these questions, you should get help.  You may not be able to solve the problems at home.  But you can get help for yourself.

There are many trained people who understand family problems.  They know what you are going through.  At school, for example, you can talk to the nurse, social worker, counselor, or psychologist. Maybe you would feel comfortable talking with your family doctor or clergyman.  Talking can help. The more you understand, the better you will feel. There may be *support groups* in your area that deal with problems just like yours.  Remember: *Don't let other people's anger bring you down!* Even the family you love must not be allowed to hurt you.

# Chapter 5

# Staying in Control

Let's review some things about anger that we have talked about in this book:

- Anger is a reaction to people, places, and things that you dislike.
- All people feel angry from time to time.
- The more emotional you are, the stronger your reactions may be.
- Anger can help you. It can motivate you to change things for the better.
- Anger can hurt you. It can lead to destructive behavior.
- Anger should be expressed in acceptable ways. You **must not** hurt yourself or others.

The most important thing to remember is to keep your anger under control. *Control* means

being able to stop yourself even if you don't want to.
*You* must be in the driver's seat. No matter who is
around or what is being said, *you* must make your
own decisions. Only you are responsible for the
way you express your anger.

Is staying in control a problem for you? Read
the following questions. Answer them on a separate sheet of paper. See what your responses tell
you about yourself.

**1. Who makes you the most angry?**
( )  parents
( )  siblings (brothers/sisters/stepsibs)
( )  teachers
( )  friends
( )  strangers

**2. How do you usually respond when some-
one makes you angry?**
( )  keep your feelings to yourself; don't let
      them know
( )  walk away; find someone to tell about it
( )  tell them off; say whatever you feel
( )  try to hurt them physically
( )  take it out on someone else
( )  plan to get even

**3. How does your response make you feel?**
( )  better, more calm
( )  wishing you had the nerve to say what
      you really feel

( )    confused, unable to think clearly
( )    ashamed of yourself, guilty
( )    nervous, afraid

**4. What would you like to change about the way you express anger?**
( )    nothing
( )    fight with words, instead of with your fists
( )    not let things bother you so much
( )    express your feelings more openly
( )    stay in control

Have you learned anything new about yourself? Are you pleased with your answers? It might be helpful to ask these questions of someone you admire. Compare your answers. Then ask yourself what you can do to work on your self-control.

## Attitude

Attitude is another name for the *mood* you are in. This "frame of mind" affects how you look at things and how you feel about them. If your attitude is good, you will be able to find something positive in almost every situation.

*Tommy had a good night's sleep and a great break-fast. He is prepared for his history test today. He feels proud of himself. Tommy hardly notices how noisy and crowded the bus is this morning. His friend saved him a seat. They tell each other jokes on the way to school.*

Working hard to develop a skill or talent can bring great personal satisfaction.

*Jimmy overslept and almost missed the bus. He skipped breakfast and forgot his notebook at home. Jimmy complains that the bus is louder than usual today. He fights his way down the aisle to find a seat. He sits frowning all the way to school without saying a word to anyone.*

Which boy started his day in a better mood? Which boy was bothered more by the noisy, crowded bus ride? Two people having the same experience can feel very differently about it. A lot depends upon their mood at the time.

During adolescence, boys and girls very often change moods quickly. Sometimes they can't explain why. Trying to see the "bright side of things" may help you react in positive ways. It's not always easy to do. It takes some practice.

Here is a simple exercise to get you started. On a separate piece of paper try to finish the following sentences with positive thoughts. (Example: I failed my driver's test last week, but I can still <u>take it over again next month</u>.)

1. I broke my ankle during practice, but I can still

_____.

2. My best friend is moving, but I can still

_____.

3. My parents don't pay attention to me, but I can still _____.

4. I don't get good grades, but I can still

_____.

5. I don't have a steady boy/girlfriend, but I can still _____.

How did you do? Did you think of something good to say for each?. Maybe this way of thinking will help. If you can remain hopeful and cheerful when things get rough, it will be harder for your anger to take control.

## Helpful Hints

Controlling your anger *is* possible. You can do it. You may find these suggestions helpful.

- *Be aware of your anger.* Learn to recognize what happens to you as you become angry. See what it does to your body. Are you grinding your teeth, making a fist, feeling tightness in your neck or stomach? Is a headache starting? Is your heart beating faster?

Maybe you do things when you are angry that you don't normally do. Overeating, smoking, or drinking are some things people do when they are angry. Maybe you become sarcastic and make fun of those around you. Whatever happens, pay attention to it. Tell yourself that it is happening because you are feeling angry. You may lose control if you don't pay attention to your anger. Angry feelings can build up inside you and get even stronger. Someday that built-up anger could explode without warning.

• *Plan ahead and stay in control.* You know yourself pretty well. Make a list of things that you are sensitive about. Think about the things that bother you. Are you upset by an alcoholic parent, a handicap, or an illness in the family? Include in your list the people who can "push your buttons." Who really gets to you? Who or what makes you feel threatened?

With this information you can do some planning. You can think of ways to handle stressful situations *before* you are in them. Knowing some things to say and how to act may reduce your fear. It may also help you control your anger.

• *Know your limits.* Just how much can you take? How long can you hold yourself back? It is important to find out. Then you will know when it's time to walk away and cool off. Leave before you do something that you will be sorry for.

• *Go to the source.* It may be better for you to tell the person who is responsible how you feel: "I am angry because . . . ." or "It made me mad when you . . . ." This can start people talking. Sometimes it clears the air. You might come to an understanding. The anger that you feel may disappear.

• *Keep trying and be prepared for some failures.* Don't give up on yourself. You will "blow it" once in a while. Everybody does. The important thing is to understand why you lost control. Ask yourself what you should have done instead.

Seeing your good points helps you maintain a positive image.

You must decide that you want to be in control of your anger. Take responsibility for how you express your feelings. And start practicing the things you can do to calm yourself down. Maybe it's a few words to yourself: "This is not a big deal." Whatever it is, try to remember to use it as much as possible. Then start working toward your goal.

Doing something positive, such as helping others, can improve your outlook and make you feel good about yourself.

# Chapter 6

## Feeling Good about Yourself

Y ou can expect to feel angry from time to time. Remember, anger is a normal reaction to certain things, or people. Each experience with anger will be different. Many things affect the way you feel. Your self-esteem is probably the greatest influence.

*Self-esteem is how you feel about yourself.* With positive, healthy self-esteem you feel worthwhile. You believe that you make a difference. With negative, low self-esteem you feel unimportant. You think everyone else is better. You believe everyone else is more valuable than you. Low self-esteem can make you unfriendly and angry. Some people with low self-esteem can become violent when they are upset. (See the section in Chapter 3 called "Anger Turned Inward.")

How do you know if your self-esteem is low? The following self-esteem test will give you some idea.  Answer the questions as honestly as you can. Think about how you feel *most* of the time, and don't rush your answers.  Responding too fast often means answering the way we *want* ourselves to be, not who we really are.

---

**TEST YOUR SELF-ESTEEM**

On a piece of paper, write a **yes** or **no** after each question.

1.  Do you like yourself?                          yes   no
2.  Do you believe in your own ability?
                                                   yes   no
3.  Do you think that others like you?   yes   no
4.  Do you take helpful criticism well?  yes   no
5.  Do you like to meet new people?      yes   no
6.  Do you look forward to new experiences?
                                                   yes   no
7.  Do you give yourself credit when you do some thing well?                        yes   no
8.  Are relationships important to you?
                                                   yes   no
9.  Are you open about your feelings?   yes   no
10.  Are you happy for others when they do well?                                    yes   no
11.  Do *you* make yourself happy?          yes   no

If you answered "yes" to most of these, your self-esteem is probably in good shape. If you answered "no," your self-esteem most likely needs some improvement.

## The Hardest Fight of All

Don't wait any longer! Start feeling great. Use these tools to build your self-esteem:

- **Look at yourself honestly.** "Tell it like it is." Make a mental list of your good points and your bad points. Look at who you really are. Be proud of your good qualities. Admit what you need to work on.

- **Stop putting yourself down.** You don't need to hear "I'm stupid" or "I never do anything right." Turn those words around. Tell yourself, "I'm not a good reader, but I'm good with numbers" or "Sometimes I have to do something over again before I get it right."

- **Accept the things you cannot change.** You want to be tall and beautiful like a model. But you are 5' 2" and average looking. So why waste time and energy complaining? Be proud of what you *do* like about yourself. Maybe you have great hair and a nice smile. Or is it your personality and good singing voice that please? Make the most of whatever special gifts you have.

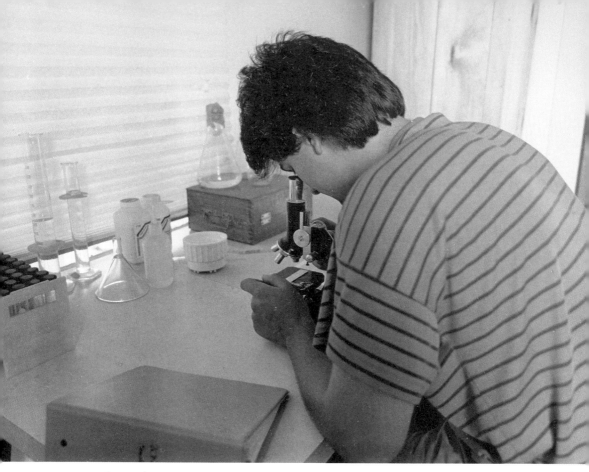

Spending time with things you enjoy—such as hobbies—
helps to improve your attitude toward life.

- **Forgive yourself.** Let it go. If you did not
handle something well in the past, it's okay. The
next time you will try to do better. Learn from your
mistakes. Remember, everyone makes them. And
most of the time you'll have another chance.

- **Start off slowly.** It takes time to make
changes. Your new way of looking at yourself will
improve with small steps. Do simple things that
you will be proud of. Visit with an elderly neighbor.
Read a bedtime story to your kid sister. Begin a
regular exercise program. Write that thank-you
note you have been putting off.

- **Be good to yourself.** If you start to feel sad, do something that you enjoy. Do whatever makes you feel good: lifting weights, shooting baskets, or drawing. (My grandmother would go out and buy a new hat whenever she needed a lift!)

Spending time with someone you feel close to is another good idea. A friend or relative can often give you the pat on the back you may need.

## Conclusion

Improved self-esteem will take you through many rough times. It does not solve every problem. But it helps you to cope with any problem. It helps you become better able to manage your feelings. You stay in control.

When you are feeling good about yourself you treat others in a better way. You have more patience and understanding. The normal ups and downs of life will not bother you as much. It's okay for some things to go wrong. You can handle that. You may not even get angry.

High self-esteem will also make you less vulnerable. That means you are not as easily hurt or threatened. It is like a "protective coating." It shields you from the effects of other people's anger.

Remember, there *is* help available if you have a problem with your anger. People *do* understand and are willing to listen. But you must take the first step. Do something good for yourself . . . see yourself as a winner!

# Glossary—*Explaining New Words*

**abuse**   The use of violence or emotional pain to control another person.

**acceptable**   Recognized or agreed to by others.

**adolescence**   Period of growth between childhood and adulthood, from about age 11 to 21.

**angry**   Feeling or showing that you are not pleased about something.

**communication**   Sharing of feelings, thoughts, or information.

**confusion**   State of being mixed up.

**criticism**   Saying what is good or bad about something or someone.

**depression**   Feeling very low.

**destructive**   Causing damage.

**embarrassment**   A feeling of discomfort or shame.

**emotions**   Strong feelings.

**express**   To say or to show.

**frustration**   Sense of being upset or discouraged.

**fury**   Anger so intense that the person seems to be crazy.

**gesture**   A movement of the hands, head, or other parts of the body that shows what a person is thinking or feeling.

**gossip**   Talk or rumor about others that is often untrue or unkind.

**grudge**   A longstanding feeling of anger, resentment.

**influence**   To change or have an effect on.

**injustice**   Unfairness or wrongdoing.

**motivate**   To cause a person to take action.

**negative**   Bad or undesirable.

**paranoid**   Thinking the world is against you.

**positive**   Good or desirable.

**rage**   Violent and uncontrolled anger.

**reckless**   Acting quickly without being careful.

**responsibility**   What someone must take charge of; a duty.

**sarcasm**   Sharp or nasty remark that hurts or makes fun of someone.

**self-esteem**   How you feel about yourself.

**sensitive**   Aware of the way you and others feel.

**sibling**   A brother or sister.

**"silent treatment"**   Not talking or communicating with someone on purpose.

**stress**   A feeling of pressure or strain.

**suicide**   The act of taking your own life.

**support group**   People with the same kinds of problems who meet to help each other.

**temper tantrum**   An outburst of anger, usually not lasting long.

**threat**   The possibility that some harm might happen.

**trait**   A recognized quality.

**transferring aggression**   Being angry at one person, but taking it out on another.

**victim**   A person who is the object of a crime or abuse.

**violence**   The use of physical force to injure or abuse.

**wrath**   Violent anger that is meant to punish or get even.

# Where to Get Help

Talk with any responsible adult you know and trust. This might be a family member, neighbor, friend, teacher, school social worker, counselor, doctor, or religious advisor.

In the **yellow pages** of your local telephone book you will find listings for:
- Counseling services for individuals and families
- Mental Health Centers
- YMCA/YWCA
- Social Service Organizations
- Psychologists

Write to:
**National Association of State Mental Health**
1001 Third Street, S.W.
Suite 115
Washington, DC  20024

**National Self-Help Clearinghouse**
City University of New York
33 West 42nd Street
New York, NY  10036

# For Further Reading

Platt, Kim. *The Ape Inside Me.* J.B. Lippincott Company, 1979; 117 pages. A young boy gives his uncontrollable temper a separate identity and learns to control it.

Riley, Jocelyn. *Only My Mouth Is Smiling.* William Morrow and Company, Inc., 1982, 222 pages. The story of a teenager who hides her fear and anger in order to survive in her family.

Schleifer, Jay. *Everything You Need to Know about Teen Suicide.* Rosen Publishing Group, New York, 1988; 64 pages. This book deals with the facts and feelings of suicide. It also alerts the reader to warning signs of suicide.

Stark, Evan. *Everything You Need to Know about Family Violence.* Rosen Publishing Group, New York, 1989; 64 pages. This book explains the pain and fear of families in trouble. It tells how and why violence starts and what can be done to stop it.

Wilt, Joy. *Handling Your Ups and Downs.* Educational Products Division, Word, Inc., Texas, 1979; 127 pages. In simple language, the basic human emotions are identified and explained. It teaches children some ways to cope with their feelings.

# Index

**About the Author**
Renora Licata is a freelance writer who has worked with children of all ages. For several years she tutored high school students enrolled in the Head Start Program. Her special interest, however, is early childhood development. Presently, she lives in Connecticut with her husband and three children.

**Acknowledgments and Photo Credits**
Cover photo by Chuck Peterson.
Photograph on page 56: Mary Lauzon. All other photographs by Stuart Rabinowitz.
Art on page 17: Sonja Kalter.

Design/Production: Blackbirch Graphics, Inc.